CYCLING
CORNWALL

Tony Farnell

Tor Mark

Published by Tor Mark Ltd,
United Downs Industrial Estate,
St Day, Redruth, Cornwall TR16 5HY

www.tormark.co.uk

Published 2018
This reprint 2021

ISBN 978 0 85025 476 1

Printed and bound in the UK

IMPORTANT
INFORMATION

SAFETY
Although the majority of roads used are country lanes or B roads and have been selected because traffic flow is very low, Cornish lanes can present their own unique problems of which you should be aware. Most are narrow, single track and winding with high Cornish hedges and no verges. Just because you have not seen a car for the previous twenty minutes, does not mean that there isn't one coming around the very next sharp corner, so you need to be prepared to stop if necessary to allow the car to pass safely. This is especially important if you encounter a bend on a steep downhill section where you may be travelling surprisingly fast, and find a vehicle coming in the opposite direction and filling the whole of the available road space. So, keep your speed under control especially if approaching a bend on a downhill slope. Unavoidably, some of the routes cross main or busy roads. In each case, great care is required, as you may encounter heavy or fast-moving traffic. If in doubt, dismount and push your bike across the road.

BICYCLES
It is important that your bicycle is well maintained, and in particular, the brakes. If you are hiring bicycles from a reputable bike hire company, they should take care of this for you; if you are borrowing bikes or using your own, you do need to ensure they are in good working order. Each route gives an indication of the most suitable type of bike - mountain, road, hybrid or cyclocross.

PUNCTURES
Punctures are an inevitable part of cycling, so you should always carry at least two spare inner tubes of the correct type for your bike, and/or a puncture repair kit. You will also need two or three tyre levers to remove your tyre from the wheel rim and a pump to inflate your replacement inner tube once it is in place. Remember, if you have a puncture without a repair kit, you may end up pushing your bike a long way! Many towns have bike shops in case you need emergency assistance with unexpected mechanical problems.

CLOTHING
If you do not cycle frequently, you may not realise the importance of warm, preferably windproof clothing, in all but the hottest weather conditions. Even on quite a warm day, cycling along at 5, 10, 15 miles per hour can produce a noticeable wind chill factor, and this becomes even more pronounced going downhill because you are going faster but doing less work to produce body heat. Equally, sunscreen is always a good idea.

FACILITIES

Facilities you may require, such as car parking, bike hire, toilets, shops, cafés and public houses, are indicated on each route. Many cafés are open all year, but inevitably some close in the winter months or operate restricted hours or days.

ROUTES

Each route is described by means of an accumulated mileage, a description and illustrated by a profile and a map. You may find it helpful to take the appropriate Ordnance Survey map to supplement your navigation. The 1:50,000 Landranger Series 200, 203 or 204 are particularly good. A bike computer will allow you to keep an accurate check on your progress by comparing your current mileage with the accumulated mileage in the text. There is also an indication of the general nature of the route, together with the suggested suitable bike type and time likely to be taken at different average speeds. The mileage, estimated time and the profile may be used to select a route suitable for your fitness, experience and time available.

NATIONAL CYCLE ROUTES

Sustrans is a national charity dedicated to developing and signposting safe cycling routes nationwide, marked by distinctive blue directional signs. Some of the routes in this book follow sections of national cycle routes and the blue signs can be used to simplify navigation.

PARKING

Car parking is specified at or near the start and finish of each ride by means of a postcode and an Ordnance Survey grid reference. Although some of the car parks are free, others require payment. If you have a long or high vehicle you are advised to check beforehand whether the car park is suitable.

SYMBOLS

Ⓟ Parking	🚻 Toilets	☕ Café
🏛 Public House	🛍 Shops	🚲 Bike Hire
🔧 Bike Shop	⚠ Danger	⸸ Signpost

INTRODUCTION

The aim of this book is to provide a variety of types of bike rides in west and central Cornwall for everyone. About half of the rides are on traffic free trails, which may appeal more to inexperienced cyclists and family groups, while the remainder are road rides, utilising mainly quiet Cornish lanes, which might be favoured by more confident cyclists, be they enthusiasts or commuters.

Both trail and road rides form a network across Cornwall, visiting towns, villages and places catering for a variety of different interests. Many of the routes have been subdivided so that sections can be completed as self-contained short rides, or added together to build up longer rides. For more ambitious riders, different routes can be joined to extend or make the ride circular. Where the rides are between two points, out and back, the routes are described in both directions, making it easier to use with different start and finish points.

When planning your rides, you need to realise that, although Cornwall is not a mountainous county, it is exceedingly hilly. The hills are not long, but they are frequent, and they can be steep. Fortunately, most of the traffic free trails are based on former railway tracks or along valley bottoms making them flat or very gently undulating. However, a number of the road rides will include at least one serious hill. Wherever possible I have tried to ensure the hill comes at the beginning, when you are freshest.

Wherever you ride, there are a few things to keep in mind if you wish to have stress-free cycling. The Important Information provides a few thoughts on how to make the most of your rides. With all outdoor activities, a few simple words will suffice: be safe, sensible and enjoy!

Tony Farnell

CONTENTS

TRAFFIC FREE TRAILS (GREEN)

PAGE

1 / **PENROSE TRAIL** (4.8 MILES) FLAT / UNDULATING — 8

2 / **GREAT FLAT LODE TRAIL** (7.5 MILES) UNDULATING / HILLY — 10

3 / **MINERAL TRAMWAY TRAIL** (11 MILES) FLAT / UNDULATING — 14

4 / **PENTEWAN TRAIL** (3.8 MILES) FLAT — 17

5 / **COAST AND CLAY TRAIL** (12 MILES) HILLY — 19

6 / **CAMEL TRAIL – PADSTOW** (12.8 MILES) FLAT — 22

7 / **DUNMERE TRAIL** (6.8 MILES) FLAT — 24

ROAD RIDES (BLUE)

8 / **HAYLE – MOUSEHOLE** (12 MILES) FLAT — 29

9 / **MARAZION – PORTHLEVEN** (10 MILES) UNDULATING — 32

10 / **HELSTON – FALMOUTH** (12 MILES) HILLY — 34

11 / **FALMOUTH – TRURO** (18 MILES) HILLY — 36

12 / **ST AUSTELL – BODMIN** (14 MILES) HILLY — 40

13 / **PERRANPORTH – PORTREATH** (12 MILES) HILLY — 44

14 / **PORTREATH – HAYLE** (10 MILES) UNDULATING — 47

TRAFFIC FREE TRAILS

1 / **PENROSE** TRAIL

DISTANCE: 4.8 miles

TIME: **60 minutes** (at 5 mph), **30 minutes** (at 10 mph), **20 minutes** (at 15 mph)

SURFACE: Mixture of tarmac, stone and gravel tracks

TERRAIN: Flat, with some undulations and a hill entering and leaving Porthleven

BIKE: Mountain, hybrid, cyclocross

PARKING: Boating Lake car park, Helston TR13 8SG, Kitto's Field car park, Porthleven TR13 9JA

OPINION: This is a great trail for beginners and families, with the bulk of the route being traffic free and flat. The route wends its way through the wooded Penrose Estate, along the shores of Loe Pool, past the historic Penrose House, onto the coast at Loe Bar and along the cliffs to Porthleven. Additionally, there are numerous alternative trails in and around the Penrose Estate; a map is available at Penrose House.

HELSTON - PORTHLEVEN

No. on maps

0.0 mi Start Boating Lake Helston ⓟ 🚻 🍴 🚲 🚵 GR SW653270
Cross the bridge over the River Cober on the west side of car park and join the cycle/foot trail

1 1.2 mi Pass gates by lodge house

2 1.4 mi Turn left towards Penrose House

3 1.5 mi Pass Penrose House ⓟ 🍴 GR SW642256

4 2.7 mi Pass the gates by the lodge house (turn left for Loe Bar Beach)

5 3.1 mi Turn right up the gravel track

6 3.3 mi Turn left at the T- junction

7 3.5 mi Turn right onto Coopers Lane

8 3.6 mi Turn left at the junction and proceed downhill

9 3.7 mi At bottom of the hill turn right at the T- junction

10 3.9 mi Turn sharp right up Cliff Road to follow the one-way system, keep left and join Peverell Terrace to pass 🏛, then turn sharp left down Salt Cellar Hill and proceed along the harbour side

4.2 mi Finish Porthleven Harbour ⓟ 🚻 🍴 🏛 🛍
GR SW628258

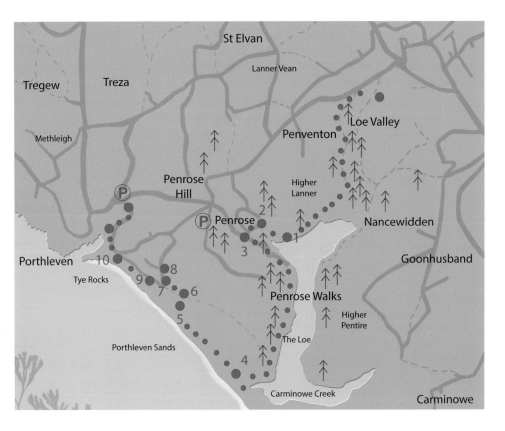

PORTHLEVEN - HELSTON

0.0 mi Start Porthleven Harbour ℗ 🚻 ☕ 🏛 ⌂ GR SW628258 Leave along Harbour Road, pass the clock tower and pier, and continue up Cliff Road

10 0.3 mi Fork right along Loe Bar Road

9 0.5 mi Turn left up the the unnamed lane

8 0.6 mi Turn right onto Coopers Lane at the T- junction

7 0.7 mi Turn left through the gate onto a gravel track

6 0.9 mi Turn right and descend the gravel track to cliff top

5 1.1 mi Turn left and follow the track along cliff top

4 1.5 mi Pass gates by the lodge house (or fork right for Loe Bar Beach)

3 2.7 mi Pass Penrose House ℗ ☕ GR SW642256

2 2.8 mi Turn right at the T- junction

1 3.0 mi Pass the gates and lodge house

4.2 mi Finish Boating Lake Helston ℗ 🚻 ☕ 🚲 🚴 GR SW653270

2 / **GREAT FLAT LODE** TRAIL

DISTANCE: 7.5 miles

TIME: **1 hour 30 minutes** (at 5 mph), **45 minutes** (at 10 mph), **30 minutes** (at 15 mph)

SURFACE: Mixture of tarmac, gravel and stony tracks

TERRAIN: Flat and undulating with one big ascent and descent

BIKE: Mountain, cyclocross

PARKING: Heartlands car park, Pool TR15 3QY

OPINION: This is quite a challenging route in places, with some steep ups and downs and some stretches of rough track. However, the views across St Ives Bay from the top are worth the effort. Near Carnkie you can join the Mineral Trail to link up to the Devoran - Portreath Mineral Tramway (see page 14). There is an alternative start and finish point car park at GR SW683395 TR16 6JS, which would allow you to miss out the busy urban section immediately around Heartlands.

CLOCKWISE ROUTE

0.0 mi Start Heartlands Pool Ⓟ 👫 ☕ GR SW667411 (clockwise route) Turn right onto Station Road

1 0.1 mi Straight on at the mini roundabout

2 0.2 mi Turn right at the T- junction

3 0.2 mi Turn left at the traffic lights, cross the railway bridge and follow the road around the left bend

4 0.3 mi Cycle straight on when the road bends right (✝ Great Flat Lode), then fork right up Chapel Hill where the road becomes a rough track, before taking the tarmac cycle trail

5 1.4 mi Fork right up the stony track

6 1.9 mi Turn left at the track crossroads and descend to the road

7 2.0 mi Turn left down the road

8 2.3 mi Turn sharp right up the rough track (✝ Great Flat Lode) to a road

9 2.9 mi At the T- junction with road cycle straight across into Copper Lane

10 3.0 mi Turn right up the rough track (⊤ Great Flat Lode)

11 3.9 mi Fork left and pass through Basset Mines Tramway Tunnel

12 4.0 mi Cycle straight across the lane following the track around the car park Ⓟ GR SW683395 TR16 6JS

13 4.1 mi Turn right to pass through the ruined mine buildings

14 4.5 mi Turn left at the road junction into Treskillard and cycle straight on at the crossroads onto a rough track

15 4.6 mi Fork right before Lower Grillis Farm

16 5.0 mi Turn left at the T- junction onto the road

17 5.1 mi Cycle straight on up the rough track as road bends left

18 5.4 mi Turn right down the rough track

19 5.6 mi Cross the road ⚠ onto the track passing King Edward Mine Museum on your right

20 6.0 mi Turn left at the T- junction with the road and then turn immediately right

21 6.1 mi Fork right at the Carn Entral sign, STEEP DESCENT to road ⚠

22 6.5 mi Cycle straight across road ⚠, across the bridge before turning left and following road/track

23 7.0 mi Cycle straight across at the road ⚠ onto track (⊤ Great Flat Lode)

24 7.1 mi Turn right before the old bridge over the railway

25 7.2 mi Turn left at the road

26 7.2 mi Turn left onto the track (⊤ Great Flat Lode), and at the T- junction with the road, turn left ⚠ over the railway bridge

3 7.3 mi At the traffic lights turn right

2 7.3 mi Turn left into Station Road

1 7.4 mi Cycle straight on at the mini roundabout and turn left into Heartlands

7.5 mi Finish Heartlands Pool Ⓟ 👫 🚻 GR SW667411

CARNKIE

ANTI-CLOCKWISE ROUTE

0.0 mi Start Heartlands Pool Ⓟ ♦♦ ☕ GR SW667411 (anti-clockwise route) Turn right onto Station Road

1 0.1 mi Cycle straight on at the mini roundabout

2 0.2 mi Turn right at the T- junction

3 0.2 mi Turn left at traffic lights, cross railway bridge and turn immediately right along track (♱ Great Flat Lode)

26 0.4 mi Join the road ⚠

25 0.4 mi Turn right onto the track (♱ Great Flat Lode)

24 0.5 mi Turn left at the old bridge crossing the railway

23 0.6 mi Cycle straight across the road ⚠ through the gate and onto a gravel track which eventually becomes tarmac

22 1.2 mi Cross the stream and road ⚠ and climb a very steep tarmac path

21 1.6 mi At the track junction keep left

20 1.7 mi Turn left onto the road, then immediately right onto a track (⊤ Great Flat Lode) to pass King Edward Mine Museum on your left

19 2.1 mi Cross the road ⚠ onto a track (⊤ Great Flat Lode)

18 2.3 mi At the track T- junction, take the left-hand route

17 2.6 mi Join the road and continue straight on

16 2.7 mi Turn right onto the track (⊤ Great Flat Lode)

15 3.1 mi Join the road and proceed through Treskillard

14 3.2 mi Turn right up the track (⊤ Great Flat Lode)

13 3.3 mi Pass through the ruined mine buildings and turn left

12 3.6 mi Turn left after passing between old mine buildings, follow the track around the car park ℗ GR SW683395 TR16 6JS and cross a lane

11 3.8 mi Pass through Basset Mines Tramway Tunnel and cross the lane

10 4.8 mi Turn left onto Copper Lane

9 4.9 mi At road junction cycle straight across onto the track (⊤ Great Flat Lode)

8 5.5 mi At junction with road turn sharp left

7 5.8 mi Turn sharp right onto the track (⊤ Great Flat Lode)

6 5.9 mi At track crossing turn right

5 6.4 mi At junction with tarmac cycle trail turn left and continue until it be comes a rough track, then a road, keep right and proceed downhill

4 7.2 mi At junction with road turn right ⚠ take care and follow road over railway bridge

3 7.3 mi At traffic lights turn right

2 7.3 mi Turn left into Station Road

1 7.4 mi Straight on at mini roundabout and turn left into Heartlands

7.5 mi Finish Heartlands Pool ℗ †† ☕ GR SW667411

VIEWS FROM ACROSS ST IVES BAY

3 / **MINERAL TRAMWAY** TRAIL

DISTANCE: 11 miles

TIME: **2 hours 10 minutes** (at 5 mph), **1 hour 5 minute**s (at 10 mph), **45 minutes** (at 15 mph)

SURFACE: Mixture of mainly gravel and stone tracks with some quiet tarmac lanes and cycle paths

TERRAIN: Flat and gently undulating

BIKE: Mountain, cyclocross, hybrid

PARKING: The Beach car park, Portreath TR16 4NQ, By-pass car park, Devoran TR3 6PG

OPINION: One of my favourite off-road routes. This is an historic purpose-built coast-to-coast trail along an old mineral railway. Most of it is traffic free and gradients are generally gradual. There are numerous refreshment facilities along the way and you can nip in for a swim at Portreath. From Twelveheads you can divert to the Mineral Trail link, which connects you to the Great Flat Lode Trail, (see page 10).

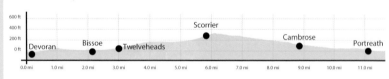

PORTREATH - DEVORAN

0.0 mi Start Portreath Ⓟ 👬 🚻 🚲 🛍 🏛 GR SW653453 From Ⓟ turn left on B3300 Redruth Road and then fork left along Sunnyvale Road

1 0.6 mi Fork left onto Mineral Railway Trail

2 1.1 mi Cross lane ⚠

3 1.9 mi Cross lane ⚠

4 2.3 mi Cross road ⚠ at Cambrose to turn left along tarmac cycle/footpath, passing 🚲 on left

5 2.9 mi Turn right at junction into lane

6 3.1 mi Straight on ⚠ at crossroads

7 3.3 mi Straight on ⚠ at crossroads onto track

8 4.9 mi Turn left up cycle track, then right at T- junction with road onto tarmac cycle/footpath and cross bridge over A30 dual carriageway

9 5.1 mi Cross road ⚠ to turn left when cycle path ends, proceed under railway bridge, turn right ⚠ at 🏛 and proceed through car park

10 5.4 mi Cross road ⚠ and turn left onto cycle/footpath

11 5.5 mi Turn right at crossroads, staying on cycle/footpath

12 5.7 mi Cross road ⚠ onto tarmac cycle trail and proceed through Unity Woods

13 6.6 mi Join lane

14 6.7 mi Straight across ⚠ at crossroads

15 6.8 mi Turn right at T- junction down short hill and turn left at bottom and proceed down Poldice Valley

16 8.2 mi Join road at Twelveheads ☕ GR SW759422 straight on

17 8.4 mi Turn left onto trail

18 9.0 mi At Bissoe ☕ 🚲 🚲 GR 769415 turn right on road ⚠, cross bridge over Carnon River and turn immediately left onto track

19 9.5 mi Cross lane ⚠

20 10.1 mi Cross lane ⚠

21 10.7 mi Cross road ⚠

22 11.0 mi After passing under road bridge, turn right to car park

11.1 mi Finish Devoran Ⓟ 🚻 🏛 GR SW790394

DEVORAN - PORTREATH

0.0 mi Start Devoran Ⓟ 🚻 🏛 GR SW790394 Turn left out of Ⓟ

22 0.1 mi At T- junction turn left on track to proceed under main road bridge

21 0.5 mi Cross road ⚠

20 1.1 mi Cross lane ⚠

19 1.7 mi Cross lane ⚠

18 2.2 mi At Bissoe ☕ 🚲 🚴 GR 769415 turn right on road ⚠, cross bridge over Carnon River and turn immediately left onto track

17 2.8 mi Turn right onto lane

16 3.0 mi Straight on taking track as lane bends to the right at Twelveheads ☕ GR SW759422 climbing gradually up Poldice Valley

15 4.4 mi Turn right at T- junction, up short hill, and then turn left onto lane

14 4.6 mi Straight across ⚠ at crossroads

13 4.7 mi Fork left onto track and proceed through Unity Woods

12 5.5 mi Cross B3298 ⚠ and follow cycle/footpath

11 5.7 mi Turn left at crossroads and stay on cycle/footpath

10 5.8 mi Cross road ⚠ at cycle crossing into 🏛 car park. Proceed through car park and turn left onto road ⚠

9 6.0 mi At T- junction cross road ⚠ and turn right on cycle/footpath and cross bridge over A30 dual carriageway

8 6.2 mi Turn left onto cycle track, and then turn right at bottom of slope

7 7.8 mi Straight on ⚠ at crossroads onto lane

6 8.0 mi Straight on ⚠ at crossroads

5 8.2 mi Turn left at T- junction onto cycle/footpath passing 🚲 on right

4 8.8 mi Cross road ⚠ at Cambrose to turn right, then immediately fork left along track

3 9.2 mi Cross lane ⚠

2 10.0 mi Cross lane ⚠

1 10.5 mi Turn right into Sunnyvale Road, then right again onto B3300

11.1 mi Finish Portreath Ⓟ 🚻 ☕ 🚲 🚻 🏛 GR SW653453

PORTREATH

4 / PENTEWAN TRAIL

DISTANCE:	**3.8 miles**
TIME:	**43 minutes** (at 5 mph), **22 minutes** (at 10 mph), **14 minutes** (at 15 mph)
SURFACE:	Mixture of tarmac, gravel and earth road, track and path, muddy in places after rain
TERRAIN:	Downhill out of St Austell, then flat
BIKE:	Mountain, hybrid, cyclocross
PARKING:	Priory Road car park, St Austell PL25 5AB, Pentewan car park, Pentewan PL26 6BX
OPINION:	This is a great introductory ride for beginners or novices which is well signposted. It's flat and traffic free, apart from the uphill drag into St Austell, but you can always miss this bit out if you don't feel like it! There are refreshment alternatives at Pentewan and a beach if you fancy a swim.

ST AUSTELL – PENTEWAN

0.0 mi Start St Austell GR SX013524 Join cycle/footpath at junction of Sawles Road and B3273

1 0.4 mi Fork left onto lane at sewage works

2 0.6 mi At end of lane, fork right onto tarmac cycle/footpath

3 1.1 mi At junction, turn left onto lane, then right onto track

4 1.4 mi Turn right into lane and left onto track

5 1.7 mi Fork right just before gate into Peckhill Wood and follow St Austell River downstream.

6 2.3 mi Pass Ⓟ on right

7 2.6 mi At bridge, straight on (turn right over bridge for Lost Gardens of Heligan and Mevagissey)

8 2.8 mi Fork left into woods

9 3.6 mi Just past turn left at T- junction onto West End road and proceed into Pentewan

3.8 mi Finish Pentewan GR SX017472

No. on maps

TRAIL 4

PENTEWAN – ST AUSTELL

0.0 mi Start Pentewan Ⓟ ♌ ☕ 🏠 🚲 🏛 GR SX017472 Take West End road out of centre

9 0.2 mi Turn right at 🚲 onto trail

8 1.0 mi Join track and follow St Austell River upstream

7 1.2 mi At bridge, cycle straight on (turn left over bridge for Lost Gardens of Heligan and Mevagissey)

6 1.5 mi Pass Ⓟ on left

5 2.1 mi At track junction turn left

4 2.4 mi Turn right into lane followed by left onto track

3 2.7 mi At junction, turn left onto lane, then right onto tarmac cycle/footpath

2 3.2 mi Leave cycle/footpath and bear left onto lane

1 3.4 mi Turn right just past sewage works onto cycle/footpath next to B3273 towards St Austell

3.8 mi Finish St Austell Ⓟ ♌ ☕ 🏠 🏛 GR SX013524

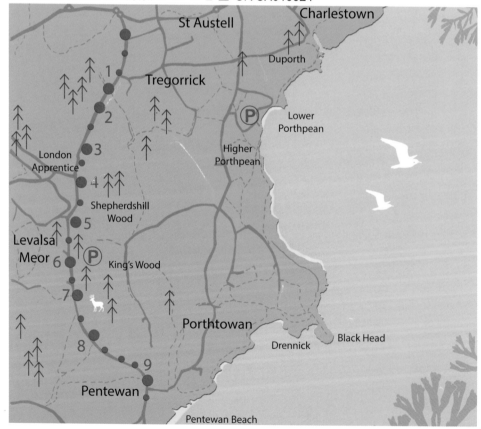

5 / COAST AND CLAY TRAIL

DISTANCE: 12 miles

TIME: 2 hours 30 minutes (at 5 mph), 1 hour 15 minutes (at 10 mph), 48 minutes (at 15 mph)

SURFACE: Mixture of tarmac and gravel road, track and path, muddy in places after wet weather

TERRAIN: Very steep hill out of Mevagissey and long steady climb through St Austell and clay hills

BIKE: Mountain, hybrid, cyclocross

PARKING: River Street car park, Mevagissey PL26 6EU, Eden Project car park, Bodelva PL24 2SG

OPINION: This is a ride of many contrasts, starting at the working fishing port of Mevagissey and finishing at the spectacular domes of the Eden Project. In between you have some steep hills, a flat valley ride on the Pentewan Trail, a traverse of St Austell town centre and a climb up the summits of the historic clay hills with spectacular views across moors and coast.

MEVAGISSEY – EDEN PROJECT

0.0 mi Start Mevagissey ⓟ 👬 ☕ 🛍 🏛 GR SX014448 Leave in St Austell direction on B3273 River Street

1 0.3 mi Fork left onto track to pass Sports Centre and follow track up steep hill (⚠ - **BEWARE** bikes coming fast downhill)

2 1.9 mi At T- junction turn right under bridge (or turn left for The Lost Gardens of Heligan) and follow track downhill and then parallel to B3273

3 3.0 mi Cross B3273 ⚠, follow cycle/footpath beside road, then turn right to cross St Austell River bridge

4 3.2 mi Turn left and follow Pentewan Trail signs towards St Austell

5 5.0 mi After passing sewage works on left, turn right onto cycle/footpath alongside B3273

6 5.4 mi At St Austell 30mph signs, turn right into Sawles Road

7 5.7 mi At T- junction turn left up Sawles Road

8 5.8 mi At traffic lights straight on to continue uphill on Sawles Road

9 6.0 mi Turn left into Eastbourne Road

10 6.2 mi At traffic lights, straight across onto bike path and East Hill

11 6.3 mi St Austell Church Street ℗ 👫 🚲 ☕ 🛈 🏛 GR SX013524 Continue around the church into Market Street, then turn left up Market Hill and continue uphill on North Street

12 6.4 mi After crossing railway bridge, turn left into Tremena Road

13 6.6 mi As Tremena Road bends right, turn left onto cycle path

14 8.0 mi At junction straight on ☂ Clay Trails Eden Project (turn sharp left to visit Wheal Martyn Clay Mining Museum) and continue climbing, following signs for Clay Trails Eden Project

15 9.0 mi Cross bridge over A391 and follow signs to Clay Trails Eden Project through former clay pits, then descending

12.0 mi Finish Eden Project ℗ 👫 ☕ GR SX048547

EDEN PROJECT – MEVAGISSEY

0.0 mi Start Eden Project ℗ 👫 ☕ GR SX048547 From bike park follow signs Clay Trails St Austell mainly climbing uphill

15 3.0 mi Cross bridge over A391 and continue following signs for Clay Trails St Austell

14 4.0 mi At track junction fork left ☂ Clay Trails St Austell (fork right to visit Wheal Martyn Clay Mining Museum) and follow track downhill

13 5.4 mi Join Tremena Road

12 5.6 mi At junction turn right, cross railway bridge and proceed down North Street, turn left, down Market Hill, at bottom turn right into Market Street, and follow road around church into Church Street

11 5.8 mi St Austell Church Street ℗ 👫 🚲 ☕ 🛈 🏛 GR SX013524 Turn right along East Hill and onto bike path

10 6.0 mi At traffic lights, straight across into Eastbourne Road

9 6.2 mi At junction keep right into Sawles Road and proceed downhill

8 6.4 mi At traffic lights straight on to continue downhill on Sawles Road

7 6.5 mi At bottom of hill turn right

6 6.8 mi At T- junction, turn left onto bike/footpath alongside B3273

5 7.2 mi Fork left at sewage works and follow Pentewan Trail signs towards Pentewan

4 9.0 mi Turn right to cross bridge over St Austell River (☂ Mevagissey and Heligan), then turn left onto cycle/footpath, alongside B3273

3 9.1 mi Cross road ⚠ and take cycle/footpath (╪ Mevagissey/Heligan) proceeding uphill

2 10.2 mi At top of hill pass under bridge and turn left ╪ Mevagissey (or straight on for The Lost Gardens of Heligan) and follow track down steep hill (⚠ - control your speed)

1 11.7 mi Pass Sports Centre on right and join River Street ⚠ into town
12.0 mi Finish Mevagissey ℗ ♦♦ ☕ 🏛 GR SX014448

EDEN PROJECT

MEVAGISSEY HARBOUR

THE LOST GARDENS OF HELIGAN

21

6 / CAMEL TRAIL

DISTANCE: **12.8 miles**

TIME: **3 hours** (at 5 mph), **1 hour 30 minutes** (at 10 mph), **50 minutes** (at 15 mph)

SURFACE: Mixture of tarmac and gravel track

TERRAIN: Flat apart from steady climb from Dunmere to Bodmin and gentle climb from Dunmere to Wenfordbridge

BIKE: Mountain, hybrid, cyclocross, road

PARKING: Link Road car park, Padstow PL28 8AY, Fore Street car park, Bodmin PL31 2DB

OPINION: Without a doubt this is the best cycle trail in Cornwall. It is purpose-built with numerous refreshment opportunities, and flat apart from the grind uphill from Dunmere to Bodmin centre, but you don't have to do this bit if you don't like hills! You can follow National Cycle Route 3 through Bodmin to Lanhydrock House and Gardens, where there are several off-road trails.

PADSTOW - BODMIN

No. on maps

0.0 mi Start Padstow ℗ 👫 ☕ 🛍 🚲 🚲 GR SW919751 Leave along Riverside passing National Lobster Hatchery and join Camel Trail

1 1.0 mi Cross bridge over Little Petherick Creek

2 2.0 mi Cross Oldtown Cove

3 2.6 mi Cross Pinkson Creek

4 5.2 mi Pass under Wadebridge by-pass viaduct

5 5.7 mi Wadebridge ℗ 👫 ☕ 🛍 🚲 🚲 GR SW990724

6 7.2 mi Cycle past Shooting Range Platform

7 9.0 mi Cycle past Grogley Halt

8 9.8 mi Cycle past Camel Valley Vineyard

9 10.4 mi Cycle past Nanstallon Halt ☕

10 10.8 mi Cycle past Boscarne Junction

11 11.1 mi Cycle past Dunmere Halt

12 11.2 mi Dunmere ℗ 👫 🏛 GR SX047676 Follow trail uphill (🚏 Bodmin)

13 11.3 mi At fork straight on (or sharp left for Wenfordbridge)

14 12.3 mi Join Scarletts Well Road, pass Bodmin Jail and proceed along Berrycoombe Road and Pool Street

12.8 mi Finish Bodmin Ⓟ 🕴 🍴 🏠 🚲 🚲 GR SX072671

BODMIN – PADSTOW

0.0 mi Start Bodmin Ⓟ 🕴 🍴 🏠 🚲 🚲 GR SX072671 Leave along Pool Street, Berrycoombe Road and Scarlett's Well Road, passing Bodmin Jail

14 0.5 mi Fork left to join trail and proceed downhill

13 1.5 mi At fork straight on (or right for Wenfordbridge)

12 1.6 mi Dunmere Ⓟ 🕴 🏛 GR SX047676

11 1.7 mi Cycle past Dunmere Halt

10 2.0 mi Cycle past Boscarne Junction

9 2.4 mi Cycle past Nanstallon Halt 🍴

8 3.0 mi Cycle past Camel Valley Vineyard

7 3.8 mi Cycle past Grogley Halt

6 5.6 mi Cycle past Shooting Range Platform

5 7.1 mi Wadebridge Ⓟ 🕴 🍴 🏠 🚲 🚲 GR SW990724

4 7.6 mi Pass under Wadebridge by-pass viaduct

3 10.2 mi Cross Pinkson Creek

2 10.8 mi Cross Oldtown Cove

1 11.8 mi Cross bridge over Little Petherick Creek

12.8 mi Finish Padstow Ⓟ 🕴 🍴 🏠 🚲 🚲 GR SW919751

7 / DUNMERE TRAIL

DISTANCE: 6.8 miles
TIME: **1 hour 20 minutes** (at 5 mph), **45 minutes** (at 10 mph), **25 minutes** (at 15 mph)
SURFACE: Gravel track
TERRAIN: Almost flat with a very gradual rise from Dunmere to Wenfordbridge
BIKE: Mountain, hybrid, cyclocross, road
PARKING: Borough Arms car park, Dunmere PL31 2RD, Snail's Pace Café car park, Wenfordbridge PL30 3PN
OPINION: This is a delightful wooded and rural valley route, following the river. Refreshment is available all the year at Dunmere and seasonally at Wenfordbridge.

DUNMERE - WENFORDBRIDGE

0.0 mi Start Dunmere ℗ ♦♦ 🏛 GR SX046675

1 0.2 mi Follow trail uphill towards Bodmin and turn sharp left (✝ Wenfordbridge)

2 3.2 mi Straight across road ⚠ at Hellandbridge

3 5.3 mi Straight across road ⚠ at Tresarrett

4 6.2 mi Straight across road ⚠ and pass disused factory

6.8 mi Finish Wenfordbridge ℗ ♦♦ ☕ 🚲 GR SX085751

WENFORDBRIDGE - DUNMERE

0.0 mi Start Wenfordbridge ℗ ♦♦ ☕ 🚲 GR SX085751

4 0.6 mi After passing disused factory, straight across road ⚠

3 1.5 mi Straight across road ⚠ at Tresarrett

2 3.6 mi Straight across road ⚠ at Hellandbridge

1 6.6 mi At junction turn sharp right (✝ Wadebridge)

6.8 mi Finish Dunmere ℗ ♦♦ 🏛 GR SX046675

TRAIL 7